Honeysuckle

Meagan Ruby Wagner

At Rest

There was
near my childhood home
a tree
boxelder, I think
that grew in the middle of a clearing
that we mowed short each summer.
We would traipse down the lane
on summer afternoons
with picnic baskets
stash our bikes among the honeysuckle
lie in the tall grass
sip on purple clover
under its branches.
In middle school
when people became too much
I would hide in the woods after school
and name the honeysuckle
and greet that old friend
still there, shade unchanged.
It is still there
though the grass has not been cut short
in a dozen summers.
I wonder, can I be buried there someday?
It is probably against some code
to lay old bones beneath older branches
but, God, it would feel like coming home.

Honey

I dropped a jar of honey once.
The floor was covered with
shards of glass and a
pool of thick sugar.
I cleaned and cleaned, and even after all the
sharp bits were wiped up and thrown out,
the stickiness remained.
All sweet.
Memory is like this.

Summer Magic

There is a
Special magic
On early summer evenings
All firefly and mourning dove
Watermelon and haze
Crickets and cicadas
Sun that seems to never set
And I don't ever want
To leave

Honeysuckle

I could not
Remember
What fed my obsession
Why honeysuckle kept creeping up in the margins
The same way it creeps through the forest
And then I smelled some
And thought:
This.

Ache

It is important to remember
(I remind myself)
That having a childhood
Worth mourning
Is a luxury.
This ache is a gift.

Priorities

I have work to do
But first
Let me wiggle my fingers
In the still warm dirt
Beneath my tomatoes
That already hang heavy and green
On the vine.
There are things to do
But before that
I must attend to the sunset
Which has selfishly demanded witness

Flex

There is a tree
Next to our drive
That drops hundreds of pinecones
In our yard
And rains pollen for
One week each spring

And on stormy nights
I lie awake
And wonder if it will fall
Smashing through glass and timber
And kill us all in our beds

Even on the worst nights
While we huddle in our basement
With flashlights and ratty old blankets
It does not fall
The branches, they do not break

Someday I want to learn to bend like that

Swing and a Miss

I sent off a poem to be published by a magazine
That promised to get back to me sometime between
Tomorrow and eight months from now.
It was a good poem.
But at the last second they asked for a cover letter.
I had not prepared one and found
I could not muster one from my dusty brain.
It's like this:
I can climb around in the trees
Finding little fruits and tossing them down to a boy with a
Basket to do with as he pleases but I do not know the
Method of boiling and straining that fruit into jam.
I do not have that recipe.
That jam would be garbage.
And so I wrote:
This is a poem I wrote. Perhaps you'll like it.
Also, maybe not.
So I suppose this is the story of how I did not get published.

Drama Queen

Everytime I write
I wonder if that is it:
If all the words are used up
And my brain is shot
And I will never come up
With anything good
Or worth reading
Ever again.
And I pity myself for a minute
And mourn my short-lived
Stint as a wannabe writer
And curse my wrung out mind.
Then I pull myself together and
Go outside/do the laundry/make some bread
And eventually
The words come back
Like the sun in the morning
Or rain in April
As if to say
Calm down
No need to fret
The world does not revolve around you.
Now pick up that pencil
And get to it,
Drama queen.

Again

I spent my childhood
Running through the woods
In strappy sandals
All sunburn and bug bite
With my sisters, three,
And neighbors, two.
We would spend hours
Sunup to sundown
Wading in muddy creeks and
Crawling like Mowgli
Hands and feet
Through the tangled underbrush.
These were the best days.
For years, when I was older
I could see only the poison ivy and thorns
And I would wonder how we ever did it?
How we made it through unscathed?
But last week, with my son
I saw, again, the tunnels
Through the honeysuckle
And wanted, again,
For a moment
To run.

These Women

Once, when someone several times removed from me died unexpectedly
I rushed to the grocery store and bought bricks of Velveeta,
boxes of pasta, a whole flat of cream of mushroom soup.
I cooked mac and cheese in massive disposable
tin pans and lined them on the counter like a funeral procession.
When I finished, I was surrounded by midwestern pasta and thought,
what on earth did I just do and why?
Now I know: muscle memory. This is what the women I am from do.
When life and death are pinched together in close quarters
These women show up with food enough for five thousand.
They will not be caught unprepared with the
multitudes on a hillside, reliant on some stray boy's old lunch.
And while last breaths rattle, these women are elbow deep in dishwater,
packing the fridges of the dying with tiny portions of casseroles
that will outlast them. These women have a million trusty recipes on stained
index cards that they break out like mourning songs when death is on the prowl.
When the wagons are circled, these women bust out their 9 x 13 Pyrex and
get to work. When I got married, one of these women bought me glass
measuring cups and said, "you'll use them," and she was right.
I want to be one of these women.

Uncaged

I worked, once, with all men
And always told my friends that
I liked it-
No drama
Not catty like women
No whispered gossip.
Now I wonder how women have earned
These descriptors
Because women are also
In my experience
The ones who show up, the ones who stay
Strong, steady, and present.
I think of a story my dad told me once
About a dog on his old farm
Saint Bernard, I think,
That spent its life caged
And how, in its former home
It was malnourished and how
Boys would walk past on their way home from school
And poke sharp sticks through the fence.
It learned scarcity and meanness
To snap and to snarl
And one day, nearly tore the arm off
A man who was painting the fence.
She had to be put down after that.
I wonder how fast she would have run

If she had been
Uncaged.

Nah

In college
When I was 17 going on 18
There was a boy
Who made sure to let me know
How I ranked in comparison to the other girls on campus.
I took notes
And did my best
To contort into a shape not my own
But I still failed that course.
I have never been much of a contortionist.
(Thank God, Thank God)
He casually bragged about his ACT score
Which I had easily beaten
But I kept my mouth shut.
I had already learned that boys like him
Did not appreciate being outdone
By girls like me.
The only time I ever heard my mom swear
Was when she said
He sounds like a real ass
And wouldn't you know it
Mom was right.
And then I think of my daughter
(Her name means "battle maiden")
Now listen up, sweet girl:
Don't you dare

Make yourself small or silent or
Rearrange one single cell of yourself to
Suit some dumb boy's idea
Of what it means
To be a woman.

A Girl's Best Friend

A diamond is a chunk of coal
That did well under pressure
Said Kissinger
But I am not some dusty rock buried in
Wavy veins beneath the earth
And I did not sign up to be suffocated
For ten thousand years
Just to be sliced and polished.

Other Girls

You're not like other girls
He said
In a meant-to-be compliment
That was all backhanded slap
Because what he meant was
Not like your sisters/mothers/daughters
And this is no gift
As though holy fire could possibly be cheapened
By makeup and acrylic nails
As though I should thank him for the distinction
And never settle too much into my womanhood
But boy, you've got it all wrong,
This isn't a mask
This is war paint
And we're coming for the boys like you.

Viper

Not all snakes are vipers
But if I handed you a barrel
Of writhing wriggling bodies and said
Nine out of ten of these guys are
Harmless as a fly
Would you thrust your arm to the bottom
Of the barrel without a care?
Not unless you had a death wish.
And if I said, well, the ones who
Kill, drip poison from hideaway fangs,
Are just bad apples, not the norm
Would you let them slither through
Your hair like Medusa?
And the anecdote about apples
Goes on to say that the bad ones--
Unless they are chucked into the
Compost to decompose and be forgotten--
Will spread their rot like poison tentacles
Throughout the whole bunch until
Bad apples are all that's left.
And while you tweet all day about
"Not all men," please know
That what you are really saying is
"Not all men are creeps, but I am one
Of the ones you've got to watch out for,"
And know now that I will not smile and play

Russian roulette every time
I pass a man on the street
Just to help you turn a blind eye
To the vipers among you.

Simone

Too good
You're too good
They told her
(We told her)
And it wouldn't be fair to the others
If we were fair to you
So please, entertain us,
And we will give you
Exactly nothing in return
Keep going
Keep going
Never stop
Not for a second
Because we need you
Need your body
For our entertainment
Just like we need
LeBron and Kaepernick
For our entertainment
(As long as they're silent)
Not slave labor
Not anymore
But please entertain us
And keep your mouth shut
Give us your body and never complain
While we demand more and more

And while your brothers die in the streets
While we refuse to give credit
While we talk about blessing
As though blessing weren't stolen goods
So shut up and entertain us and
Never speak up
Never speak at all
We still need your body
Differently now that a century and a half ago
But we'll use you up
Thanklessly
Just the same

Sister

That's my dress
What'd you do with my makeup
Get out
So annoying
Leave me alone
Please leave me alone
Make her leave me alone

Oh nothing
What are you doing
Want to come over
Can you come over
Can I come over
Can you hold the baby/cut my hair/help me cope

Here, this would look good on you
Come sit close
Let me braid your hair
And while we weave
Tell me what breaks your heart
And fills your soul
And I'll tell you mine

Home

12 years ago
(Give or take a few months or weeks or days)
We went on our first date
Which was, if I recall,
Driving around town in your old Jetta
Laughing a little too eagerly
Both wearing false confidence and
Carefully rehearsed nonchalance
Like a brand new jeans with premeditated worn out knees
But we were both nervous.
Tonight, a hundred thousand hours later
We went out again
Ate nachos and drank beer
And spoke of old dreams and new hopes
Hand in hand
A few hours stolen away from the chaos
And sticky hands that wait for us at home.
And after all these years
I am still so glad
It is you.

Chosen

Love is not always
A reaction
A response
A feeling.
Not Casablanca
(All drama and beauty)
Because while I did like that one
It doesn't exactly end well
For the lovers.
More often, it is an action.
All verb.
A million tiny favors
That all add up to
Chosen.
It would make a lousy movie
But I'll still spend all my money on tickets
As long as you go with me.

Attachment Issues

I knew a girl in college
Who told me once
When we were dreaming out loud of after
That she only wanted
To marry a pastor
And I gaped, horrified
That in her wildest dreams
She was only an attachment

Anniversary

This year we opted for a quiet dinner in
Chipotle and cheap wine
And in the earlier years I might have thought this
Sad (a giving up)
But now I know it as a settling in
Of the best sort.
There was a fight early on
When you left and walked
In the rain
And I followed you
Now I would let you go
And wait for you on the porch with
A peace offering.
We have learned how to argue
How to go to bed angry
And wake up less so
Learned that tension
Like smoke
Dissipates with fresh air and time
Learned (are learning) the contours
And edges of each other
The sharp places and soft spots
And even now
We are just getting started.

Places We Could Go

Meet me outdoors
In the hazy summer dusk
Inky greens and salmon skies
Cricket song and birdcall
And sit a while
Here on the porch
Barefoot
Drink in hand
Side by side.
Barely an inch between
And let's just listen
For a moment.
We have an hour or two
If we're lucky
Before the kids start their
Cycle of alternate waking.
Just think of the places we could go.

Safe

Yours was the first face
Our babies saw
When they were push-pulled
Out into the world
And I think of how terrifying
Birth must have been for them
All pain and cold and unknown
And I think of seeing you at the end of all that
And think
Thank God
That you are there
Theirs

Baby C

My arms are sweaty where your
Weight sits
But I dare not move
Because your milky breath
Is slow and steady now
You smile for a second in your sleep
And then get back to your rhythmic snoring
I am hot and achy
But I dare not move
Because soon you will wake
And the day will begin
All noise and shouting over broken snacks
And this moment will be over
So nestle close, baby
I don't mind the ache

Not a Cricket

Mama, do you hear
That noise? Those
Are crickets.
I tried to make a song
Like a cricket
I tried and tried
But I couldn't do it.
Because I am not a cricket.
I am a human boy.
Sometimes
I hear them from my bed
At night and I think
They are trying to talk to me
Maybe tell me stories or something
But I don't know
Because I am not a cricket.
I am a human boy.

Soak

Soak it up!
Soak it all up!
They tell the young mothers
As though we are unaware of
The lightning fast passage of time
The way hours evaporate
As though we ever think of anything other than
How our children need us a little less each day
Or the fact that they will
Never again
Be as small as they are right now
As though we do not mourn
Every article of outgrown clothing
That we pack away in plastic baskets
That turn basement shelves into catacombs
As though we do not lean on
Pantry doors and weep at the brevity of it all
As though exhaustion and gratitude
Were mutually exclusive.
But also,
Too much soaking is just drowning
And there are days when
I would saw off a limb
With a pocket knife
For just five minutes of quiet.

Mother's Prayers

I am seldom certain
How to pray.
For every miraculous healing:
There are ten thousand
Untimely deaths.
For every portion of daily bread:
A dozen bellies
Distended with hunger.
For every answered mother's prayer
Whispered in desperation
In the dead of night:
A mother's grief.
For every mother the world over
Lies awake at night
Begging for their children's lives:
That they will grow old and
Turn grey and earn wrinkles.
That God will spare them addiction
And mental illness
And cancer
And tragedy.
Sometimes God does
And sometimes God doesn't
And it is not for lack of mothers' prayers.
For every moment of speechless joy
Its negative, speechless with sorrow.

Mostly I just curse under my breath and call out
Oh God
Oh God
Oh God.
And maybe there is no one there to hear
And maybe there is
But I can't help the calling out
Anyway.
And maybe this is faith:
Less certainty (or no certainty)
And more calling into the void
Betting/begging against all odds
That someone is listening.

Undoing

They tell you
Before the baby comes
That you'll never sleep again
But what no one mentions
Is that you will find thousands of new
Ways to worry
And scores of terrors to keep you up at night.
They don't tell you how your whole body will ache
Not only from birthing and nursing
But also from the growing:
How every packed away size feels
Like suffocation,
Every summer gone by
Like a ton of bricks on your chest.
How your body will mourn each passing day.
They don't tell you about how you'll lose yourself
And the guilt you'll feel for wanting to be found.
How you will be torn in two
By the wanting.
Drowning in the space between never wanting to miss
A single second and wanting a fraction of one of those seconds
To thrust your head above water and breathe.
They don't do justice to the ferocity of love
Which is less pink hearts
And more raging animal-
A violence to it.

And they say that perfect love casts out fear
But mother's love invites it
Breeds it
In tsunamis, not tidal waves.
Nothing neat about it.
They don't tell you how you'll be completely undone,
And welcome the undoing.

Things I Tell My Children

Sometimes I lie awake at night
And worry I will run out of time.
I'll fall down the stairs and break my neck
Or cells will turn aggressive, abnormal,
And that will be that.
Poof.
Gone.
I worry I will not get a chance to tell my children the things they need to know
Like:
It is always worth it to root for the underdog &
Take a deep breath before you open your mouth &
What other people think about you is none of your business.
Drink water &
Wear sunscreen &
If you have to fight for someone's attention
They're not worth it.
Take up all your space &
 Do not make yourself small or silent &
Choose the kind boy who makes you feel at home in your own skin.
And most of all
I love you
I love you
I love you

And even if I lived a hundred thousand years
I would still run out of time
To tell you how much.

Full

Summer afternoons
Were mostly spent
Shelling peas
And stringing beans
On the front porch
With my grandpa.
We'd sit there in the shade
For hours
Shelling and stringing
While mowers hummed
In the background
Toes digging in the dirt off
The side of the porch
Eating every single piece
As we worked.
When we finished
We had nothing to show for it
But tired fingers
And full bellies.
Motherhood feels like this most days:
All wrung out with nothing accomplished
But full bellies.
Turns out that is enough.

Father

Once
When a friend was sick
And I did not know how to help
I called my dad to see if he could
Send me the name of a doctor.
Instead, he said
Hang tight, kiddo,
And he walked out of a business lunch
And drove straight there.
He drove us to the hospital
And sat in the emergency room
For hours
Into the early morning
Just shooting the breeze.
When I was all panic and fear
He said
Hang on
And he showed up.
This is what it is to be a father.

Mom

My sisters and I used to tease my mom
Mock her for the ways she warned us
Incessantly: Girls, (she'd say) Girls, listen,
No matter what
Never do crystal meth or take in a sex offender
For a roommate or hitchhike in the dark across
Nebraska or go cliff diving in shallow water or
Take drinks/food/candy from a stranger
In a van or wander down dark alleys at night or
Fall in with the mafia, the men who bet on horses
Or do cocaine off dirty bathroom floors
Never drink rubbing alcohol
Or eat undercooked pork
And never smuggle drugs for the cartel
We'd say Geez, Mom, who do you think we are?
And now I know we were her blindfolded babies
Helpless as ducklings
Walking through a field of landmines
While she sang out warnings from behind

Other People's Children

There is no such thing
As other people's children
Is one of the things Glennon taught me
And so when my maternal instincts kick in
And I am tempted to gather my children in my arms and
Knit them in tight
I must remember that this is how we will sink
Like cannonballs
Straight to the bottom of the lake.
I must remember that what is good for my neighbors
Is good for my children
And that it my children prosper at the expense
Of the neighborhood
I am just delaying and expounding the
Price my children will pay
For their ill-bought security
And that there is no such thing as
Good for me if that same thing is not good for all
And that if I want to save my children
I must resist the urge to gather tight
Sequester and alienate
And instead reach out for something to hang on to
And if we could all do that
Open ourselves and link our arms
Imagine the safety net we could knit for our children.
Imagine the world they could create.

Extra and Ordinary

I do not
Most often
Meet God
In the places God is supposed to dwell
But in the muddy outskirts:
In the woods among the pines and honeysuckle
Backyards over glasses of wine and
Ugly truths
Sunday mornings at home
In nowhere near my Sunday best
On broken curbs
And the parts of town dubbed "rough"
God comes to me in tiny kindnesses:
A stranger who picks up my child's pacifier
A mother who smiles as my child wails at the grocery store
An old Sikh man who sets down his garden rake
And cheers as I run, painfully slowly, past
Shared meals and gifted pasta
Friends who do not mind the mess
I used to wonder why
But now I know
God lives here
In the extra and ordinary spaces

Girls' Night

We sit cross-legged
On living room floors
Yours, this time
Mine, next
And trade little pieces of ourselves
Hand to hand
Laughing and weeping
Interchangeably/simultaneously
Over growing children and
Long gone childhoods and
The lies we have believed
We offer up news of ourselves like small offerings:
We are still/he is not/I am still/I never was
I started/I quit/I want/I need
And nod along together in solidarity
Like a buoy on the waves
That bears witness to the incoming tide
As if to say
Yes, yes, yes
Tell me more next month
When we sit cross-legged
On living room floors

Genesis

God must be up there looking down shaking Her head
And clicking Her tongue at the multitude of ways we have
Misunderstood Her, making swords out of plowshares
And twisting and warring over words meant as poetry.
Arguing over six literal days and natural selection
And missing the point completely, which was this:
See the heavens? The galaxies? Himalayas and Appalachia?
Watch the way the bird of paradise parades and pirouettes,
And listen to the dusky call of the mourning dove .
Name the colors of the Grand Canyon or a beachy sunset.
Great Barrier Reef and Isle of Skye and Kilimanjaro:
I molded these with my old wrinkled hands and they are Good.
(And because God must have known how we'd doubt and wonder:)
Now look at your own hands, child, and knead the soft folds of your
Belly, feel the thrump of your heartbeat, put a hand on your chest and
One on your stomach and breathe. See that, daughter?
These same old hands made you, too, and You are Very Good.
Don't you forget it.

Liturgy for the Flag Removers

God our Father
Meet us in these spaces
That are holy
And wholly yours
On American soil, yes,
But soil that was first
Shawnee and Cherokee and Chickasaw.

God our Mother
God who crosses borders by night
And cradles babies in her arms
On the cold floors of detention centers
Show us our sins.
Show us the harm we have done
By both our action and inaction.
May our hearts break at the families
We have torn apart and
The neighbors we have abandoned.
May our broken hearts move us to
Tired arms and calloused hands.

Holy Spirit,
Remind us that there is
No such thing as a Christian nation.
Do not allow us to hide behind
Flags and banners of red white and blue

And disguise atrocity
And cruelty
And ignorance
And selfishness
As patriotism.

Remind us that you are not
An American God
Clothed in red white and blue
Any more than you are a
Ugandan God
Chinese God
Chilean God
Russian God
Guatemalan God.

Remind us of your teachings:
To love our enemies
And turn our cheeks
And feed the poor
And welcome the stranger.
To be peacemakers
And wound-binders
And servants.

Remind us that you walked in sandals
Not cowboy boots
And that pulling ourselves up

By our bootstraps
Was not part of the beatitudes.
There is no space for manifest destiny
In the Good News of the Gospel.

Lord have mercy
On we who have sought
Hollow solace
In the shadow of the flags
That stand (imposters)
On sanctuary stages.
May we not litter our
Sacred spaces with
The flags that we do not
(Ought not)
Worship.

Christ have mercy
On our American dreams.
Replace them with
Hunger for righteousness
And justice.
May we chase after peace
In lieu of picket fences.

Amen.

Morning Prayer

God
Help me to be less of an impatient grump than I was yesterday.
(Not 0% grump, just *less,* because I do believe in miracles,
But that would be one for the books.)
Give me today my daily bread
And my kids their daily peanut butter sandwiches.
Help them to someday eat something other than
Peanut butter sandwiches, too.
(Maybe when they turn eighteen.)
Please, Lord, have mercy and let my children outlive me.
Help me to be less self righteous
And remember that the things that
Enrage me about other people have probably just
Struck a little too close to home.
Save me from despair,
And help me to remember that you are hope
And that the thing about hope is that
It sticks relentlessly in the most unlikely of places
Like molasses in the kitchen.
Protect us today from tragedy,
Even though tragedy strikes without discrimination
And freak accidents do not heed prayers.
Forgive me my debts and remind me to
Loosen my grip on my grudges.
Jesus, be justice.
And Jesus, show me the ways I have been an obstacle to justice.

Help my children to take good naps
And be less violent with each other than they were yesterday.
For Yours is today
Yours are our minutes
Yours are our triumphs and failures.
Be close to us today.
We love You.
Amen.

Net Worth

Blessed are the poor in spirit
The poor in dollar
The poor in net worth
As though worth could be
Captured and measured in
Nets like fishes

Blessed are they who work long hours
In the heat and the cold and the dark
Bringing home not quite enough to make ends meet
Like arms around trees:
Fingers that don't quite touch
On the far side

Blessed are they who proclaim:
My hours are worthy of enough to build a life
My days are worthy of a living wage
My life is worthy of more than the bare minimum.
I am made for life to the full
Not the meager leftovers
Doled out miserly
While the powerful profit

For theirs is the kingdom of heaven
Not confined to the heavens
But on earth, too, in the thin spaces

Between clocking out and clocking back in
Heaven in the spare minutes and cents
Clawed from between the vice-like
Fingers of the rich and powerful

God who put on skin and bone
Who sweat and ate and stank
And walked in the dust
And heard the wails of the sick and poor and the dying
The outcast and the destitute
And met them with extravagance:
Hear us.

Sunday Homebodies

Blessed are the homebodies
Those who have not yet figured out
How to return to the sanctuaries
For yours is the sanctuary
Of living room couches
And front porch swings.

Blessed are the wounded
Those who have been broken
And rejected on
Hallowed ground
For yours is the healing
That defies the gatekeepers.

Blessed are the weary
Those who cannot muster
The energy to put on their
Sunday best
For yours is the
Comfort of honest existence.

Blessed are the patient
Who do not rush
Others' return
For yours is a steady peace

That waits and does not panic
Over lesser numbers.

Blessed are the naturalists
Who worship in hiking boots
Those who find God in all her
Glory in the dappled light
Between the trees
For yours is Eden.

Blessed are the mothers
Who spend Sundays
Like all the others
Fetching snacks
And being baptized in
Bodily fluids.
For you are the salt
Of the earth.

Blessed are the
Weary, the
Wary, the
Wounded, the
Homeless (physical and spiritual), the
Wanderers, the
Hesitant, the
Doubters, the
Skeptics, the

Outsiders.
For yours is the kingdom of heaven
And God will be there when you're ready.

Body

The body
In all its frality:
Bones that snap
Skin that burns
Hearts that spasm and stop
Organs themselves that fall out of place
And it is a wonder
That we keep going at all
When we are such upright
Walking-about
Medical emergencies waiting to happen
And yet we do keep going
And that is a miracle
Each step
Each beat
Each lift
Each birth
Each carry
Each digested meal
And so we give thanks
Knowing
It doesn't have to be this way

Tragedy

When I was twenty-one
And found my first wrinkle
That stayed, camped between my eyebrows
After I stopped smiling
I spent $189 dollars
On a small tube of some elixir
Made from never-spoiling French melons
And touted by a former supermodel
As magic! that kept her looking
The same for thirty years.
Imagine if we asked that of trees and mountains:
Never change
Never shift
Never soften
Never slouch
Never grow
If we begged the galaxies to hide their expansion?
What a tragedy.

Ceasefire

I wonder what age it was
Three? Five? Seven? Nine?
When I
(We)
Felt the flesh between my fingertips
(Our fingertips)
And decided to wage war?
Felt the flesh and folds of myself
(Ourselves)
And found it foreign
And decided to escape?
And why we
Expend so much energy
Shrinking and drinking
Our way out of our own skin?
And what it would be like
If we laid down our weapons and
Came back home?

Plea

Our Father who art in heaven,
Come be here, too.
We're a mess.
Amen.

Thievery

It should come as
No surprise
That we do not easily feel the
Acute grief of Palestine-
We who live on
Stolen land
Parcelled up, renamed and sold
For thirty pieces of silver.
The flower beds where I plant petunias
Were once Shawnee
Though they have been driven from a hundred thousand homes by now
And relegated to land we did not know what to do with.
This land is my land
We sang in elementary school.
What a lie.
So no wonder, no wonder
We once again struggle to see theft for what it is.
No wonder we cannot name
Atrocities when we see them.
They look like us.

Wake

Another day, another massacre
Mass casualties
Because this is America
And the stories always ask
Who was this man? and why?
And 99 times out of 100
I could tell you
He was an angry man
A loner
A history of violence & hatred of women
A trail of restraining orders and battery charges in his wake
But still, let him arm himself to the teeth
Because this is America
He did not get the girl or the promotion
He thought was his birthright &
Believe it or not, faced consequences on occasion
For the havoc he wrought &
This, he thought, was unfair
And so he demanded a thousand pounds of flesh as payment
Guns are not the problem, they argue,
But gasoline does not start fires
And still, if the sky was raining embers,
I would not campout at a gas station.
And now, this man who cursed the womb he came from
Has stolen a near dozen futures
And frozen hearts mid-beat leaving black holes in their stead

Two hands worth of wakes in his wake
But still we will do nothing to stop the next one
Because this is America.
So watch over your shoulder at:
Work/school/concerts/grocery stores/clubs/malls/nail salons
And never let down your guard
Because this is America.

Pulse

I was at the front of the sanctuary
Near the altar
When I heard the news
(Did you hear? Did you hear?)
Numbers kept spilling in
Fifteen
Twenty-six
Forty-seven
At least forty-seven
Forty-nine
Dead
Gunned down while they were supposed to be
Dancing
During Pride seemed especially cruel
Like lemon juice in a gunshot wound
And my friend
Who was supposed to pray that morning
Couldn't stop saying
Oh God
Oh God
Oh God

Lord, Have Mercy

Another execution
Scheduled murder
Going down in the USA
The land of the free and
Home of the brave
Still can't stop killing
Killing
Killing
Killing
Even though
We know
(We know)
That the ones that end up on the row
And stay there long enough to die
Are only there because the lack the
Resources to escape
Even though we have seen doomed men
Exonerated
Their long cries of "innocent!" validated
By newfound evidence.
I wonder how many innocent
We have slaughtered?
Lord, have mercy.

The Hill We Die On

A hundred thousand
Millenia
All together
The years of doctors' schooling
And virologists' education
Centuries spent poring over
Microscope slides and in ICUs
On midnight shifts
All that expertise thrown out
Because someone's aunt
Had a friend
Who had a coworker
Who had a son-in-law
Who had a bad experience
That she heard about on Facebook
(Maybe, but who even is this guy?)
And while millions around the world are dropping dead
We are throwing away our chances
Because of blog posts and Google searches
While children and chemo patients get sick and die
We sacrifice them up for the sake of our barbecues
Because we cannot bear to be inconvenienced
And somehow this has become the hill that we die on
And we never even bothered to look down at our feet
And notice the bodies we are standing on
The bodies that we crush as we dig in our heels.

Slippery Slope

I think of the things we were taught to fear:
Slippery slopes and spaghetti straps—
The way our own bodies betray us—
Double pink lines that simultaneously
Were the only important thing
And that which would ruin us—
The gay agenda
Which as far as I can tell is only:
Exist.

They never warned against the slick, slimy texture of greed.

The people who taught this fear
Were credited as wise
But I think, now, that we could replace that with
Full to the brim with privilege and power
And terrified of having to share.

Too

Listen and know
It's not just you
Everyone else
Is lonely too

Break

I see you
Gather up your anger
Like shards of broken glass
And hold it close
Enough to draw blood
And I wonder if you know
You are allowed to loosen your grip
This broken glass is not what makes you

Kool-aid

I was talking
once
about a time and place
I used to live and the listener (sort of)
said, Wow, you sound bitter
and, Lots of people liked it there, you know.
Well, poison *is* bitter
and lots of people liked jonestown
prior to the kool-aid.

Seeds

snow melts
seeds buried
planted
rain pounds dry dirt
mud splatters
seeds sprout
frost comes
seedlings die
sun shines
soil warms
nothing
nothing
nothing
seeds sprout again.

Humanity

Sometimes I am overwhelmed
By the evil and callousness
I see and think, humanity is
A lost cause.
On these days
I try to remind myself
Of exceptions to this rule:
A high school teacher who,
At the height of my anorexia,
Bought me a bag of pretzels
Everyday at lunchtime.
He always pretended he just happened to have extra change.
I always threw them away.
He kept buying them anyway.
My summer boss,
Who never mentioned
The fact that I left early
Multiple times a week for
Doctors appointments and therapy
And bought me sugar free Popsicles on hot days.
My mom, who shows up relentlessly.

And then, I have hope.

Vine

There is a climbing vine
Blue-indigo clematis
That I bought for a dollar
Off the discount rack at the garden center
When it was ninety-nine percent dead.
That was three summers ago.
It sprouted once, and was almost
Immediately weed-wacked.
Back to zero.
I was certain then that it was a lost cause.
This year, while pulling weeds from
Among the sticky stalks of Russian sage
I found it: bursting up wildly from dry, rocky dirt
That is not really suitable for life.
It shouldn't have made it.
I did my best, unintentionally, of course,
To kill it, and still:
Vine.
Hope is like this.

Breathe

When the heaviness comes
And threatens to suffocate
And the air itself seems to have had
All the oxygen wrung out of it
And just taking breath is too much
Go outside
Find a patch of dirt
Garden or flower pot or vacant lot
Get some earth beneath your nails
Rub the silt between your fingers
Lie in the grass and feel the itch of each
Broken blade and burr
Listen
Do you hear that?
Mourning dove and whippoorwill
And that scent carried on humid air?
Honeysuckle and hay
They are here for you
And you are here for them
Sit in each other's company
For a while
Until you can breathe
Again

Wait

When the darkness falls
(And it will)
Remember (remind yourself)
That this is the night
Not the end
And look for the night lights
Moon and stars
Not as sunshiney bright as the day
But enough to get you through.
Find a soft spot to settle
Beneath an old oak, nestled in the tall grass,
And watch the stars rotate overhead.
Listen to the night life that has come
To keep you company in the dark.
Breathe like labor:
In through the nose, out through the mouth,
Deep belly breaths,
Delivering yourself to another day.
Wait it out.
The sun will surely rise again.

Survival

One day soon it will surprise you
When you notice
In the space between breaths
That the things that used to tear you in two
Are gentler now
Or perhaps gone all together
The things you thought would
Certainly kill you
Have not
And here you still are:
Living.

Exodus

We did not leave
(Have not left)
Because of production quality
Or hip-ness
Or marketability
Or even the hypocrisy
(Though it was, in part, the hypocrisy)
But because questions
(Good questions)
Were met with platitudes
And because despite all the slogans,
I would not invite my gay friends through these
Heavy oak doors
And because, while I do love Jesus,
I am less and less convinced
That he resides in the puddles
Of stained glass light.
We have left to *find* Jesus
Not because we've abandoned him.

Wilderness

They readied us for battle
And taught us that the Enemy was lurking around every corner
And in every intimate crevice (especially those).
They told us that we must Know Scripture
Because we would certainly have to defend ourselves
From the hostile nonbelievers.
They warned us about slippery slopes
Becoming lukewarm and being spat out
And bemoaned all those who went before us and walked away.
Shame shame shame.
Must not have memorized enough verses to keep the devil out.
But what we found was that the enemy was lurking in the pews, too
And preaching from the pulpit
And that we were not actually under the attack we had been
Taught to fear for all those years.
(Not from the nonbelievers, at least, but there is
Plenty of friendly fire from behind church doors.)
And it was not because we were luke warm
Or not serious enough about Jesus
But because we started to notice that the places we were
Did not at all seem like places Jesus would like to spend time if he were here.
And even now people will say
Look, she walked away and now she's lost.
Tsk tsk tsk
But I'd rather be lost with Jesus in the lonely wilderness than
Safe and sound, tucked in a pew, waiting for the enemy that's already there.

Feathers and Leaves

I believe in God
And before you think me noble or naïve or good or dogmatic
Let me say
I believe in God
The way a child who has fallen into a pool reaches for a hand
Not because they know with certainty
That someone is there
But because they need there to be
In order to survive.
Because in order to put one foot in front of the other
I have to convince myself I'm walking toward something.
I could be wrong.
Sometimes I am overcome by the extremities of life:
Breath-stealing joy and bone-crushing sorrow
First breaths and last breaths, often too close together
Love and betrayal; togetherness and isolation
And we puny humans tugged back and forth
Between the two ends, quivering in the middle
And in the seconds/minutes/days/years
When I get too close to either end
I reach out of the water for God
And God meets me there
And in these moments I believe.
In these same moments
I also think of the redwoods.
Is it coincidence or divine that the mightiest trees

Grow in California, land of earthquakes and fire?
That even where the ground breaks apart beneath
Unsteady feet and threatens to swallow us whole
And fires rage like hell on earth
Life hangs on?
I think of the word flex: all muscle and sway
The balancing place between stay and go, life and death.
Emily Dickinson called hope the thing with feathers
But sometimes I think hope is the thing with leaves
And that maybe God lives there
Among the trees
In the feathers and the leaves
And beckons:
Come see.